laws
of the
jungle

Jaguars Don't Need Self-help Books

Yossi Ghinsberg

BOOMERANG
NEW MEDIA

Published by Boomerang New Media
4425 South Mo Pac Expwy., #600, Austin, TX 78735

Distributed by Greenleaf Book Group LP

For ordering information or special discounts for bulk purchases, please contact Greenleaf Book Group LP at 4425 South Mo Pac Expwy., #600, Austin, TX 78735, (512) 891-6100

Page design and composition by Greenleaf Book Group LP
Cover design by Greenleaf Book Group LP

Publisher's Cataloging-In-Publication Data

(Prepared by The Donohue Group, Inc.)

Ghinsberg, Yossi.
   Laws of the jungle : jaguars don't need self-help books / Yossi Ghinsberg. -- 1st ed.
   p. ; cm.

   ISBN-13: 978-0-9771719-1-0
   ISBN-10: 0-9771719-1-4

1. Self-actualization (Psychology) 2. Conduct of life. I. Title.
BF637.S4 G45 2006
158.1

Library of Congress Control Number: 2006931759

Printed in the United States of America on acid-free paper

06 07 08 09 10 11 12   10 9 8 7 6 5 4 3 2 1

First Edition

To my wife, Belinda Yong,
my closest friend along this
path of life, and to the
light of my eyes, my daughters,
Mia, Cayam, and Nissim.

I am the eternal traveler,
at home wherever I am and a
foreigner even where I was born.

Contents

Acknowledgments   ix

If You Want to Be Human, Be a Beast First   1

Be the Music, Not the Conductor   17

The Fig Tree Will Never Bear Mangos   37

The Seasons Always Change   59

The Cage Door Is Open   77

Evolution Is Created   97

Life Is Perfectly Perfect   111

The Time Is Now   125

The Purpose of Life Is Death   141

Acknowledgments

Laws of the Jungle began with an idea from my literary agent and very dear friend Margaret Gee. Margaret felt that in a world where anxiety often reigns, people could benefit from my perspective, and she also came up with the title of the book.

To my good friend Bharat Mitra for sharing the vision and acting on it: what goes around comes around. Special thanks also to Steven Bookoff.

My deep love and gratitude to Sensei Rohm Kest for his transformational gift of yoga. Thanks to Daniel Schreiber with whom I've discussed many of these laws and to Amir Paiss who has traveled with me on many expeditions. Love and gratitude to a very special friend Ron Fremder. Blessings to all my friends of the past, present, and future.

Finally, I'd like to acknowledge the invaluable contribution of the team at Greenleaf Book Group, in particular the encouragement, trust, and beautiful friendship of Meg LaBorde.

First Law of the Jungle

If You Want to Be Human,
Be a Beast First

The laws of the jungle are laws of nature. Minerals, plants, and animals belong to the earth. They are all nature, one and the same. They have no sense of separation from the elements, the environment, other species, or weather. We are nature. Nothing is outside of us, yet our conscious minds perceive everything as separated.

When you understand you are it, there is acceptance of it. When there is acceptance, there is peace, for sanity begins with accepting what is.

And since the conscious human mind is the only one that is not tuned in to that connection, the First Law of the Jungle states, if you want to be human, be a beast first.

a beast is nature

A drop of water in the ocean is the ocean itself. Yet this drop is holding on to its drop identity, insisting it is separated by a membrane that detaches it from all other drops and from the ocean. This is not what beasts do; this is what humans do. The conscious mind's sight is limited; it sees borders and boundaries all around and, by its own peculiar logic, concludes that reality is that of separation. Hence, it develops drop mentality and defends this mentality with its life. It has a drop ego, a drop consciousness, and its life is encased within the narrow confines of the drop's limitations.

The truth is there is no drop; there is nothing *but* ocean. With the right perspective, we can see that we are the ocean. But lacking that perspective, the conscious human mind insists it is a drop, and it cannot let go of this perception . . . unless it stops trying.

The **drop** is an illusion. Let it go, and be the **vast ocean**.

When a single country is exploding in war, the shock waves are felt across the world. Plagues are not contained by political borders. Humanity is like a single body: the individual parts mean nothing by themselves. We are all one.

Each species does exactly what it does best to survive, except for human beings. Our acquired reality is that of separation, while the truth of our existence is that of unity. We see the world as separate from ourselves and fail to live within the interconnectedness and interdependence of this world. But there are no winners unless we all win. It's time for healing, and we are all involved.

The laws of the jungle are not taught to the creatures by older generations, and the laws are not handed down to them by some great bearer of knowledge. These laws are written in the code of life itself and all living things possess the faculty to access the code, to read straight from it, and act accordingly. All living things can sense these laws because they are part of nature. They are nature. There is no separation.

Like all beasts, we must adhere to these ancient and prevailing principles of nature if we want to experience harmony within ourselves and on earth.

a beast needs no salvation

The desperation that comes with separation leaves humanity ceaselessly and obsessively looking for salvation. And as a result of living in this reality of separation, salvation too is separated from us. Hence, we look up to a god, a savior, some entity from another realm totally alienated from us, our Father in the heavens, the Messiah; and we nurture the concept of heaven and hell—both places distinctly separated from our earthly existence.

But if these places are where we ultimately belong and they are not here, then we are but transient guests on Earth. We are visitors—not part of it, not connected and dependent—merely passing through. So while we are here, we are here for the pillage.

The beast has something we've lost.

Of all the beasts, we are the only one with this prevailing sense of separation, with a notion of not belonging, with the feeling that something is wrong with us, with the idea of salvation that will come from above.

But without separation, there is no need for salvation, for there is nothing wrong with us. We are a part of this earth, we are not guests; we do not need to be delivered from this place. It is our home.

a beast is body first

A beast is perfectly attuned to the body. Yet humans live as if we are a mind and a mind only. We believe the human mind places us above all other beasts. We are enslaved to the mind, totally engrossed with it, controlled by it with no control of it.

Indeed, the mind contains tremendous practical wisdom and is responsible for the astonishing prog-ress we have made in the world. The mind is a problem-solving machine, more efficient than any computer ever developed. The mind's purpose is to do its work, to solve problems, to make inquiries, to investigate, to explore. We can praise the human mind endlessly, for it is awesome indeed.

But, being human, we give ourselves over to the rule of the mind. The whims of the mind control our lives, and we serve the mind blindly. The mind commands and we obey, oblivious to consequences, no matter how grave the price. But the purpose of the mind is to analyze, to solve problems. And when there are no problems to be solved, the mind will create them. It will tell us that we are separate from all other things, from this world. Our sense of separation is the work of the mind.

There is more to living than the realm of the mind.

We must reconnect with our bodies, the basis of our natural existence. It is the body that carries the secrets of life. The code is encrypted into our basic design, a design with purpose. If we dwell in the body, we will connect to the code, we will connect to our purpose. To see beyond the confusion of the mind, go to the body for refuge and guidance. The body is wiser than the mind, because the mind is part of the body. Abandon the mind. Remember, you are a beast before you are human, and the beast lives in the body first.

The **body is**
the **union of**
everything
that you are.

We have evolved quickly, and there is a discrepancy between our bodies and our lives. We do not hunt and gather, we do not chase or run, we do not climb trees. Our bodies atrophy and we lose access to the secrets contained within. Make time for your body. Explore it, maintain it—walk, run, climb, breathe deeply—do all of the things the body was designed to do. All beasts do what is necessary to maintain their bodies. The beast uses the body in perfect alignment with its purpose.

Do not underestimate the body.
We let our bodies go, but still want to feel good—mentally, emotionally, physically. When we feel good physically, we feel good emotionally, as do all beasts. Our emotions and mental states are tied to our bodies. Health is our main asset. When we are physically sound, we can be emotionally and mentally sound. Go back to the body; find encouragement there.

Be in the body first, for you are an animal. All of the animals around you have peace of mind; there is no schism between their bodies, their minds, their emotions, and their spirits. They are perfect unions within themselves. Trust that the design of what you are is smarter than your mind. Look to the design for answers rather than relying on the mind. Stop looking for a solution to a problem that does not exist.

Recognize that you are a perfect union, and you are a part of the world around you.

a beast knows purpose

Among beasts, there is no guilt, no remorse, and no atonement; there are no insecurities or confusion or lack of self-worth. Every animal feels right, fit, and ready for action at any given time—this is living.

How can it be that human beings are the only species so tormented and disconnected from their most natural state? How can it be that we are the species enslaved to an existence in which the wants never cease to exist while our true needs are long forgotten?

Look at the beast and see life for yourself: There is no malice in the kill, just obedience to the needs of survival, and there is no victim on the other side of it, just acceptance. There is no hatred and no bad blood, no need for revenge, and no need to stand up for transitory rights. There is no separation, only a deep interconnection as each and every species depends on another. This is the manifestation of one.

Humans are the most extraordinary creatures on the face of this planet. Indeed there is no other beast designed like us. Our potential is all encompassing, our capacity just beyond our own comprehension. What amazing specimens we are: our bodily functions, the scope of our emotions, our mind's infinite abilities, and our spiritual aptitude to lift the veil and be one with our world.

We are all that, and yet, instead of exploiting our awesome potential, we seem to be stuck in struggle and constant striving. We seem to be lacking something so fundamental—the very basic peace of mind that comes with the clarity that allows us to see our purpose, for we seem to be living in the dark.

In a fundamental crisis of
origin and purpose,
confusion reigns.

To soar above,
we need to take a
step back:

To be human, we need to be
beasts first.

Second Law of the Jungle

Be the Music, Not the Conductor

Life is music. A great symphony exists, and we are a natural part of it. All living things contribute their unique melodies, harmonies, and rhythms. Nothing is mundane, nothing is casual. Each element is precisely tuned like a musical instrument in an orchestra. If we can just accept that we are a part of this symphony, we can produce music that is harmonious, healing, and pure.

Our purpose here
is to contribute to the
fantastic music,
the **healing** music,
as all living things do.

The orchestra is cosmic and the music sublime. But can we hear anything beyond the noise and clatter of our own minds? We are vain and proud and thrive on our own self-importance. Fueled with eagerness for power and control, inflamed by shortsighted ambitions, we push and we shove and we force ourselves against the music that flows within us, trying to assume the role of the conductor. But this role was never available to us and never endowed. We are not qualified to perform the job, but we pretend that we know what we are doing. Look around and you will hear the catastrophic cacophony that we make. This is not music.

the music has no control

We are trained to gain control, maintain control, and never lose control. We feel the need to control ourselves, control others, and control our environments. We want things to go our way, to happen as we command. We want this badly, and we want it now. But the universe doesn't work this way, and our struggle for control is constant. It causes confrontations, crises, conflicts, and disillusionments that lead to the breakdown of the human psyche and soul, bodies and minds, families and societies and civilizations.

We contemporary human beings, with our remarkable achievements in science and technology, obviously esteem ourselves as the most intelligent species. At least we proclaim this as a fact. But if this is so, how can it be that we never cease to fight with each other, that we destroy our own abundant planet, exterminate its species, exhaust its natural resources, contaminate its seas, and rip holes in its atmosphere?

We manage this planet as if we are in control of it. Nobody appointed us to this role; there was never a vacancy in the first place. Everything was perfectly fine, amazingly in order, until we leapt out of our place and forgot our original role. We developed civilizations, created gods, and assumed the place of the conductor. Ask yourself: Do you like the music? Are you enjoying it? Is it soothing and healing? Maybe it is time the self-appointed conductor let go of his post.

Give up your need
        for control,
    let it go.

Be the music, not the conductor. Listen for the beautiful music that exists within you. It will guide you. Understand how your unique music contributes to the amazing symphony that is life. Understand that without your music, the symphony is lessened. Understand that when you try to be the conductor, the symphony becomes discordant.

It is scary to let go; fear strikes. But fear is the best guide. It shows you the way—always towards it, never away from it. If you run from it, it will chase you forever.

Letting go is the essence of life. One cannot hold onto anything, for nothing can be held; everything is in a constant state of flux. Letting go is the art of understanding the most basic principle of life. If you let go of your false position as conductor and assume your role as a part of the symphony, your music will be unique, flowing from all that you are, from your natural and most serene state of being.

Once you give up your need to be the conductor . . . Wow, what a sense of relief, what a load you were carrying, trying to control the uncontrollable. Your lungs fill with air now, you can breathe, and the strain on your shoulders, that constant pain you had become accustomed to, fades away. The music within you is miraculous.

the music does not resist

Most people try to avoid the pains of life. It is so futile. Adversity is part of life. Trying to avoid it will only attract more adversity. There is no place to run from adversity, but there are all the places in the world to face it.

Rather than resist adversity, cultivate an attitude of never being a victim. You will watch adversity move on. You will realize that adversity is just a temporary state. Though we are taught to resist the pains of life, by resisting them we are holding on to them.

What we resist
persists; what we
oppose grows.

As Newton's law states, for every action, there is an equal and opposite reaction. If you push against something, it pushes back with the same force. The more you struggle, the more your struggles are futile.

Nobody can avoid the turmoil of life. If we can stop our attempt to control life and simply take responsibility for the aspects of our selves that manifest in the world around us, we can act in accordance with the flow of the symphony. When you are responsible for yourself, you are not a victim. If you are not a victim, you have the power to act. You have the power to contribute your music to the world around you.

the music is innate

Tribal people in the jungles and deserts lived awe-inspired lives before we, the "civilized" ones, interfered with them and distorted their balance, bringing them our artificial laws to replace their natural laws. As if they needed our "civilized" laws and our "civilized" gods.

They lived and thrived, they were playful and sincere and tuned in to the symphony of life. They tapped into the wisdom of the universe and read from its open source. They played their music, aware of the subtle instructions of the conductor. They had fewer inhibitions, and play and laughter were major components of their lives, as were singing and dancing. We appeared and called them primitive, savages, animals. We decided that these poor beastie creatures needed our help and guidance, that they needed to see the "light" of our god. We brought them disease, we brought them poverty, we disturbed their peace, and we raped their environments. Some saviors we are.

We thought of them as animals. But many of the animals in the jungle are more enlightened than we are. What the animals all know, we have forgotten. Before we call ourselves human beings, we had better remember that we are animals first. Without this foundation, we cannot ascend to assume our role in the symphony.

Learn the music from the beast within you and ascend.

We were born to the earth, but we act as if we own it, forgetting it is our mother and that all other species are actually our brothers, cousins, and kin. We are all part of the symphony, here to play together, aware of one another and the different music we offer.

The laws of the jungle are the laws of nature itself. You are the law, and you are nature; there is no separation. The innate truth of the second law of the jungle exists within us. The player, the instrument, the music—they are all one. It is all in you; it has always been there. Why look anywhere else? You are part of it; you are it. Wake up and see the obvious: you need no guide, no map. Hone your virtues, your empathy, your awareness of the world.

Let your music play forth.

the music creates the symphony

The music within each living thing contributes to the natural state and beauty of the world. The outer world is a reflection of the inner world. If you believe yourself to be beautiful, you will project beauty into the world around you through your music. If you feel an abundance within yourself, the world will be more abundant. But if you are full of conflict, of struggle, of strife, the world around you will be full of these things also.

Your subconscious communicates with the natural world on a very basic level. This communication affects the world around you in ways that we cannot understand. Your reality becomes who and what you are.

If you **want** to **change** your **reality**, you need only look inside yourself.

In our efforts to control the world, to be the conductor, we fail to recognize that if we allow the music within us to flow with the natural symphony that is life, we will have a much greater effect on the world around us. Instead, we apply our conscious mind to molding our realities. We are manipulative and calculating. We are desperate at times and unscrupulous at others. And all of this is reflected back to us.

Two men live in the same apartment building. Their television sets bring them the same news. When they wake in the morning, the weather for each is the same. One opens his window a crack, looks outside, and growls, "Another day in hell." The other man throws open his window, inhales deeply, and exclaims, "Another day in paradise!"

What is happening in the world outside of us is simply a reflection of the inner state of humanity: separation, isolation, disease, famine, greed, war, environmental destruction. Is this who we want to be? Is this the music we want to create, discordant and destructive?

Tune in to your innate music, accept your role in the symphony, and see your world becoming one of harmony.

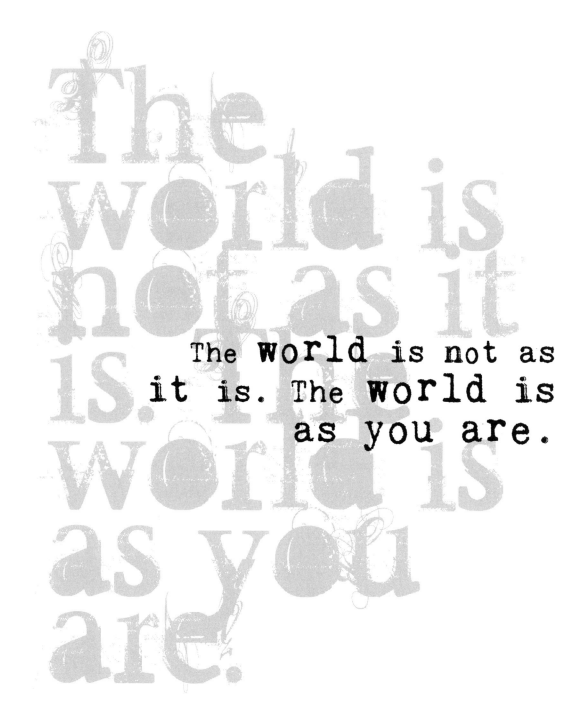

The world is not as it is. The world is as you are.

the music is harmonious

If we could wake up to the truth that reso-
nates through all that lives, wake up and dance the music that
is love, we would be filled with overwhelming gratitude, bringing a sense of wholesome spirituality to our days. We would
not need temples, mosques, churches, or synagogues—there
would no longer be any place *not* sacred. We would not follow
religions that constrain and restrict our spirits and endorse
separation from ourselves and each other.

If you desire a sense of harmony in your personal life, if you want to flow in a better rhythm and be more
in tune with your surroundings and environment, if you want to
be effective and of greater meaning to your family, workplace,
community, and society, let the rhythm of your music guide
you, and be the most harmonious music you can be.

Do not try to be the conductor; this is not your role
in the symphony. If you contribute your unique harmony, you
have done enough. Life will guide the notes you play.

Tune in to the conductor and offer your music at the right time.

We can change the world if we change the music we offer. Let the music you offer be harmonious, let it flow from you to all of the people around you. Peace activists, make peace in your hearts before you go to the streets to rally. Environmentalists, clean the rooms of your spirit before you attempt to sweep the oceans and the forests of the world. There is healing to be done, but the healing must start within you first.

Observe your need to control, and then—aware and precise, gentle and wise—let it go.

Let go of the role of the conductor and let your melody play forth.

Contribute to the sweet harmonious music that is life.

Third Law of the Jungle

The Fig Tree Will Never Bear Mangos

I once walked in the jungle east of Santa Cruz de la Sierra with Chocomono, the shaman of the Chimane people, and his youngest son, Mundake. He was a beautiful, introverted boy around seven or eight years old. He had been born with a twisted right foot that was also somewhat shorter than his left foot. He kept up with us, but it was only with great effort.

At one point, Chocomono and I leaped over a felled tree, and when Mundake tried to follow, he fell facedown onto the rotting forest floor. He cried out, and tears of frustration ran down his cheeks. I felt he was embarrassed because I, a foreigner, was there to witness his shortcoming. Chocomono sat on the log and helped his son to his feet, listening attentively to the boy's cries and complaints for a moment. He then pointed to a great fig tree that bore many figs and began speaking softly to the boy in the Chimane language. From his intonation and gestures, I could see he was telling his son a story.

After a few minutes they both got up from the log and we resumed walking. It was clear that Mundake's entire demeanor had changed. He seemed at ease, more confident, and despite his limp, he seemed to move with the effortlessness of his father.

When I asked Chocomono what had happened, he smiled and said, "The boy said he hates being crippled and as slow as he is. He asked why he couldn't be like his older brother, who is the fastest and most able of all the village boys. I told him a very old story about the fig tree that wanted to be like the mango tree, which is taller than all other trees, and bears heavy, bright fruits that taste so sweet that all toucans and macaw birds come to eat them and seed the wild mango throughout the valley. The fig tree, however, is heavy set and short, and its fruits are small and quick to ferment and rot. The fig felt inferior to the mango tree and decided that the only way it could feel better about itself was to become a mango tree. It sent its roots deep into the ground and fought all other tree roots for every trace element to gain a few extra inches in height. The fig tree worked hard day and night pushing its fronds up toward the sky until it stood taller than all the other fig trees in the jungle. It was so proud of itself. And when a passing toucan landed on the fig tree's top frond there was no tree happier in the entire forest, for it was sure it had managed to change itself completely. Then, when the season came, it flowered and young fruits started appearing on its branches. To the fig tree's devastation, they were not mango fruits but figs.

"Soon after the fig tree decided that all of his efforts had been in vain, a passing gang of spider monkeys, gathered on the strong branches of the tree, nested in its lush branches, and feasted on the fermented fig all night, becoming drunk on it and completely ignoring the shiny fruits of the mango.

"When the spider monkeys continued their travels, they carried the fig tree seeds in their bellies and spread the seeds across the Amazon basin.

"I told my son," continued Chocomono, "If you are born a fig, you will not yield mango no matter how hard you try. You may fool some for a minute into believing you have changed and become someone else, but when your season arrives, you will still be you. You can bear big, sweet figs that will ferment into an invaluable elixir, or yield shriveled bitter figs that are good for nothing. But mangos, my son, you will not yield, no matter how hard you try."

I looked back at that fig tree

that we had left behind, knowing how much Chocomono liked drinking chicha*, and I wondered if Chocomono did not make up that "old story" right then and there.

are you that fig tree?

We as humans are the most endowed and burdened of all creatures: being ourselves, what is so simple and natural to all living things on earth has become extremely complicated for us. Separating ourselves from the natural world, we've lost our sense of true identity. Not recognizing our true selves, we are often torn between what we are and what we desire to be. Thus we live our lives in great dismay.

We are the fig tree that wants to be a mango tree.

*Fermented fruit alcohol

The fig tree may not realize it wants to be a mango tree, but it knows that as a fig tree it is not happy. It has decided that something is wrong, and by becoming something else, the problem will be resolved. The fig tree decides that it needs to change. It sees that the mango tree seems happy producing mangos. So the fig tree concludes that to be happy, it must become a mango tree.

The fig tree seeks sage advice from gurus and teachers, experts in mango trees. It studies and learns everything there is to know about mango trees. It does its best to adorn itself like a mango tree. It even tries to speak the language of the mango trees.

The fig tree makes a sincere effort to become a mango tree. It may be able to fool its surroundings, and in some cases, it may even fool itself. Yet when it is time to bear fruit, the fig tree will have figs hanging from its branches not mangos.

At the **end of the day,**
and at the **end of life,**
the fig tree will
always be a **fig tree.**

If you plant a cedar tree seed, a cedar tree will grow from it and scatter more cedar seeds. If you plant corn seeds, corn plants will rise up in your fields and bear ears of corn. When you plant a fig, do not expect it to grow mangos: it is as simple as that.

It is good to be reminded of this simple truth. Explore it in your life and a process of unchaining will begin. It is more powerful and far more efficient than the futile process of trying to change and be someone else.

the fig tree knows it is a fig tree

The two most primal commands in the universe are know yourself and be yourself. All living things in nature abide by these two sacred commands; they obey the laws of the jungle and are perfectly aligned with the world. These basic concepts create the natural force of survival that leads to the evolution of all species—a natural process that makes perfect sense.

Know yourself.
Be yourself.

Human beings, however, seem to continuously work against their true nature, creating values and laws that have little to do with our innate condition. We inherently feel the discrepancy. We feel that something is wrong. Hence, we live in a state of disturbance, scattered rather than knowing where to go, insecure and confused. Eventually we decide that to feel satisfied with our lives, we must be different. We develop unrealistic expectations.

When people have unrealistic expectations, a vicious cycle controls their lives. It works like this:

Something must be wrong with me—I need to change and then I'll be happy (unrealistic expectation)—I've tried to change, but something is still wrong—it must be somebody else's fault (blame)—no, it is my fault (guilt)—I don't know whose fault it is (fear)—something is terribly wrong with me (confusion)—I'll follow that guru or religion (desperation)—something is still wrong, I'd better change . . . (gullibility)—and the spiral goes on and on.

The reason you are constantly searching is that you have unrealistic expectations, expectations created by our culture and your mind. Yet your mind keeps suggesting that the problem is somewhere outside of you. You waste time trying to alter the outside world. You get new clothing or a new nose, change your spouse and job, but you are still restless and unhappy. As long as you follow this futile strategy, there will always be someone or something else to blame.

So you fight with the outside world, which is pointless, because nothing you change in the external world will change who you are. And you live a life of constant struggle, always in strife, always in conflict, never at peace with others, never at peace with yourself.

One day you wake up to the grim realization that maybe it is not the outside world that is to blame. You have blamed everything and everybody and things are still not right. And it hits you like a bomb—if the world is not to blame, then it must be you.

The blame is transformed into guilt and you waste more time trying to fix yourself. You read books, you take courses, you find a new religion. But at the end of the day, though you may believe otherwise, you are still you, although a sadly unrealized version of you. And eventually you realize that all of your efforts were in vain, because you are still unsatisfied.

You don't know who to blame. Fear reigns. Rudderless you are ready to take on anything that will promise to deliver you from your misery. Very soon the ship is sinking, and your entire life is passing you by.

This cycle goes on and on, eventually leading to unbearable stress and unhappiness. I've met older people who never escaped the cycle, who still haven't accepted themselves for who they are after a lifelong and futile quest to become someone else.

You need to rethink your strategy.

The flaw is obvious. The initial step out of the cycle is not to try to change, but to accept who we are. In order to *accept* who we are, we need to first *know* who we are. Facing this challenge, we naturally apply the best tool we have—the mind. But the mind is the faculty least connected to our natural state. The mind is the cause of the problem to begin with, the faculty that creates the separation from our innate condition. To truly know ourselves, we must explore the question of who we are with our other faculties: our bodies, our emotions, and our spirits.

How difficult is it to just let go and be ourselves?

Look at the cycle and try to find the weakest point. Where can it be broken? At the point of initiation, at the point of expectation. If a fig tree expects itself to be a mango tree, the rest of the cycle will naturally occur.

In fact the fig tree makes no effort whatsoever to become a mango tree. It survives by knowing itself in a most basic way and by being itself. Be that fig tree; it carries all the wisdom we need. Know who you are, be the best that you can be instead of attempting to be someone or something else.

the fig tree accepts what cannot be changed

Most of us have heard the prayer, "God, grant me the serenity to accept the things I cannot change, the courage to change the things I can, and the wisdom to know the difference." There is a great truth in this prayer, yet we spend exorbitant time and energy trying to change what cannot be changed, oblivious to the things we can change and incapable of understanding the difference. Why is that?

We live in a culture that endorses this behavior, a culture that establishes celebrities as role models, supermodels as a cue for how we should look, authorities as arbiters of what is right and wrong, television therapists as healers of all our ills, institutionalized religions as deciders of what is moral and what is not, and powerful corporations as dictators of what our needs are. They are all encouraging us to be mango trees, so to speak.

Don't buy into what others tell you you should be. Why live someone else's life? Being you works better because you, in your natural state, are aligned with the laws of nature.

Your **uniqueness**
is **not a weakness.**
It is the **true source**
of your **strength.**

We have disassociated ourselves from our evolutionary connection to the natural world. We do not see ourselves for the beasts that we are. Most living things in nature accept what they are, physically and otherwise. We, in our unnatural state, seek to change ourselves, because we are told we should.

This is exactly the opposite of accepting what cannot be changed. Of course, you can force perceived change on yourself. You can change your hair color, gain or lose weight, go to a plastic surgeon. Yet did anything really change? No.

If you are insecure because of the way your face was structured by nature, will you gain security by changing your face? Maybe temporarily, but it will be fleeting. Over time, your general sense of insecurity will prevail. You will find other things about yourself that need to be changed. You will continue to look outside of yourself for acceptance that will never be found. You must look within yourself.

Accept yourself.
Your strength and
beauty resonate
from within.

Do not live by the perception that you are what other people believe you to be.

the fig tree aspires
to be a fig tree

A fig tree that has realized that it will always be a fig tree can be a spectacular fig tree. When there are no more quests for change, there is unlimited space and time to expand and grow and bear the sweetest figs possible. This is the art of realistic expectation, of recognizing oneself for what one is, of knowledge, acceptance, and growth.

There are no limits and no boundaries to growth.

The fig tree does everything it can possibly do to ensure that it is the best possible fig tree. It is awe inspiring to see how creative it can get in its pursuit of survival and making sure it supports the next generation of fig trees. It produces amazing fruits that bear better seeds than the seed it came from and develops a strategy to ensure these seeds will flourish and blossom.

Like the fig tree, know yourself, accept yourself, be yourself, and be nothing other than yourself. Put all of your energy into it. Make sure you contribute to improving the life of the next generation of your species on the planet. Sow your seeds of light. Aspire for the next generation to have a better life than yours, create the best of circumstances for them to develop in the best of conditions. Limit the pressures they will experience to be something other than what they are.

What a relief it will be to accept yourself for exactly who you are. Finally, you will find a place to rest.

What a joy it is
to aspire to
be you.

Fourth Law of the Jungle

The Seasons Always Change

I once lived in the depths of the Amazon forest for three years in a remote valley where only one indigenous tribe, the Takana, still thrived. They were isolated from other cultures and lived in accordance with their millennia-old traditions. Part of their belief system recognized that in order to survive they had to continually reinvent themselves according to new circumstances. Time and time again, I witnessed them doing that so skillfully and surprisingly unemotionally. They were quick to learn how to negotiate with the loggers, miners, government officials, and conservationists that encircled them like hungry hyenas. The Takana simply smiled subtly and applied their hunting techniques to trap their opponents at the negotiation table. They kept their cool and held their own cards close to their chests. They identified the weaknesses of their enemies, manipulated them, played them against each other, surrounded them, and attacked them from different directions simultaneously. They left their enemies baffled and disoriented like an anteater in a trap. In the end, they left the table with far more assets than their opponents ever imagined giving. I was amazed seeing these masters at work, yet I couldn't understand how the Takana had gained this tactical knowledge. One would have thought they would be naive and gullible, but if anything, they were shrewd and cunning.

Since the Takana are slow to trust strangers, it took me years before I learned their ways and their secrets. In essence they innately understand change, and they know the world as a living thing. They observe the seasons and see them change. They adapt to their environment without hesitation and accept that change is a part of life. When the big rains fall relentlessly for months on end, the lowlands are often flooded and turn into lakes, the river gushes and doesn't allow fishing, and the fields are soaked and muddy. From their simple mud and straw dwellings on top of the mountains the Takana observe nature's work and never go against it: They don't build dams and they don't carve terraces. Instead, they drink fermented maize, eat smoked meats, play music, and patiently wait for the season to change. It always does.

Years earlier, before the arrival of loggers, miners, and more recently conservationists, missionaries visited the Takana and brought with them a good-looking god on a cross. They also brought disease that eventually wiped out all but three families. These families left the village, ironically taking nothing but the church bell, moved to another territory, and started a new village on another mountain. The essence of survival is a swift and efficient adaptation to new circumstances. The dead must be buried, and the living must move on with life.

The Takana are not unique in their environment. The Amazon—in fact, the entire forest—is quick to adapt to any new situation. When the flood comes, some species migrate to the hills while others crawl, hop, or swim in ready to feast. Change is first a reality and second an opportunity. No species in the jungle complains and no species tries to hold onto the old. They are not attached to anything but the sacredness of the continuity of life. When the season changes they adjust immediately and naturally to the new situation and thrive in it. If they didn't, they wouldn't survive.

One can learn a lot from the Amazon jungle and its dwellers. The Amazon is home to almost 50 percent of the species on earth, yet there is room for all. Each species finds its own special and unique niche to make its home. No home is bigger than what is needed, efficient simplicity is the guiding line, and there is no greed. No species accumulates more that it can eat, and no species kills for ideology or fun. Resources are unlimited if one is creative, so why compete against, exploit, or deprive others?

Adaptation to change is the art of survival and survival is the only game that is played in the Amazon. All species in the Amazon are alert and vibrant, constantly attentive to the slightest fluctuation in their environment. They have very few habits and patterns to follow. Instead, they rely on sharp senses and quick assessment of new situations. A rapid decision is followed by unhesitating action. Theirs is a lesson we should all learn.

Understanding change is understanding life, for life in the universe is indeed the life of change—a constant and perpetual state of flux where there is only one stable factor: everything changes.

It is not that we need to change ourselves, although that is a prevalent illusion; rather we must understand the essence of change and align our world with it. All living things exist within the flawless flow of constant change. Surrender to the flow; trust its flawlessness.

There is a flawless flow and nothing but the flawless flow.

The great evolutionist Charles Darwin said, "It is not the strongest of the species that survives, nor the most intelligent that survives. It is the one that is the most adaptable to change." It is in your nature to survive, so adapt. Adapt and free your will to live. You were born to experience life. Wake up to the flow; give in to the flux. Do not hold on to anything; there is nothing to hold on to. The seasons always change.

Adapting to change is the essence of surviving, of experiencing happiness, of the satisfaction of success, of remaining mentally sane and physically fit. Of all species on Earth, it is only our own that has stagnated through our obsession with patterns, forms, and perceived conditions. We defend them with our lives rather than live in the moment and act according to conditions as they truly are, in the present. Yet deep inside us lives the code of life, recognition of the impermanence of all things. We only need to let it awaken within us.

Surrender and let the
wind of change blow
the dust from your eyes.

Surrender to change, for there is nothing but the flux and flow. The waves of change are titanic—resist and you will crush, crack, and break. That force cannot be harnessed or controlled or resisted—it is the force of creation itself.

seasons are bountiful, seasons are bleak

Life is challenging no matter where you are or who you are. Africa and America are not that far apart, nor are the experiences of the king and the pauper. But many people measure their realities in terms of pain and pleasure. They see the tough times as the thorny stick and good fortune as the sweet fruit. What we all need in life is balance between the stick and the fruit, and the understanding that neither will last.

Those who get too much of the stick become harsh people. They are broken, both physically and emotionally. They lose all trust in people and the world. Those who get too much of the fruit come to feel that it is never enough. They get fat and lose their agility and alertness. They believe that the fruit will always be plentiful. And when the fruit is taken from them, as it eventually is, they experience incredible misery.

We must accept that we may always get the stick and we may always get the fruit, and eventually both will pass away. Good and bad are relative and extreme. Why be split by the poles?

Walk on the
     middle path
   where it is
calm and quiet and
     everything
              is passing.

In a retreat in India I heard this story: A good father died and his two sons mourned for him. They eventually opened his dearly guarded chest. They could not find a will and testament, so they decided to divide the contents of the chest fairly and equally. At the bottom of the chest they found a small jade box, and in it, wrapped in silken cloth, lay two rings. One was of shimmering gold with a large ruby mounted like a flame. It was glorious. The other ring had no glitter. It was a simple ring made of silver. The elder brother could not take his eyes from the ruby ring. The glow from the ruby burned in his eyes as he spoke to his younger brother with conviction. "Our father must have received this ring from his own father. This must be a family treasure passed from generation to generation and harbor great significance. This tradition must be continued, and as the elder, I must be its guardian." The younger brother took one solemn look at the ruby and agreed. He quietly placed the simple silver ring in his pocket. The younger brother thought, *Father was a wise man. Why would he hide such a simple silver ring with one of precious gold and ruby? Why would he wrap them both in silk and keep them side by side in the jade box?* When he was alone, he took the ring from his pocket and turned it slowly in his fingers. As he did, he saw fine writing on the inside of the ring. Closely examining it with a looking glass, he was able to read the inscription: "This too shall pass."

Many years passed and life brought both brothers what life brings—interesting times, wars and plagues, tough years and joyful years. The elder brother grew in wealth and posture but was consumed by plans and worries. He was gray and dull-eyed, his face carved with lines of bitterness and dissatisfaction. The family treasure, that precious ring, was long forgotten. In a moment of crisis, he had sold it to the local pawnbroker. The younger brother also had a family and a variety of business endeavors; some were good, others bad. But miraculously, life seemed to leave no mark on him, grace surrounded him, he remained youthful and agile, and his smile was his trademark. Even in the toughest times, he maintained an even keel, with the silver ring always there on his finger.

This too shall pass. All things change. Even in the toughest moments, maintain a smile, even if only in your heart. Do not hold on to the fears and worries that come with bad times. Do not hold on to the elation and security that come with good times. Don't let change upset you.

Maintain an even keel,
ride on the sea of change,
and you will find
lasting happiness in life.

Happiness is found in living fully in the
moment without attachment to it. Happiness is derived from
being able to live through what happens, for nothing happens
to you and everything happens for you.

seasons are destructive

We are conditioned from the time that we are born to cling to that which is temporary, as all things are temporary. As we amass more of what we desire—money, power, fame—we feel more secure in clinging to it, believing we will always possess it. And when that false belief collides with reality, the sorrow of losing is greater than the joy of possessing. Thus you must remember this *law of the jungle*—life is about constant shift and change. How can we be called fortunate or happy if what makes us so fortunate or happy can be taken from us? We work so hard to protect ourselves from this, but it is futile. In the end, everything can be taken from us.

When you are feeling most secure, ask yourself, "What if I lost it all?" Only when you accept that this could happen at any moment will you be free and able to truly find happiness.

What you hold dearest can be taken from you at any time.

The pain of losing is greater than the joy of having it all.

If we accept that all can be lost, we let go of fear and allow joy into our lives.

seasons are fluid

To live within the constant flow of change, one needs to be as flexible as a palm tree in a strong wind.

One night on Huene, a remote, untouched island in Papua New Guinea, I was lying beneath a palm tree on the soft, sun-bleached sand. As the evening unfolded, the wind began blowing hard. Suddenly I had a realization. It was the wind that had designed the tree. The entire tree was perfectly shaped to dance with the wind, to make love to it. The tree was flexible and bent willingly to the wind. The huge fronds were cut in many ribbons, allowing the wind to blow through them. The wind could not break the tree, because it had designed it.

I have seen people broken by the winds of life. Adversity is part of life for all of us, but being a victim is always a matter of choice. Those who abide by the fourth law of the jungle are never victims. They know that life can be tough at times, and other times it can be pampering, like the waves of a great ocean.

Learn from nature. Don't stand there stiff and hard, ready to deal with any trouble from a point of inflexibility. Yield to present circumstances. Accept that they are as they are, and that they will soon change.

If you flow with them, you will never be broken by them.

The seasons always change. It is our conditioned nature to cling to passing phenomena. Observe these qualities within yourself, and bring understanding to the moment. Ask yourself, "If this will pass, if this is transient, why try to hold on to it so rigidly, setting myself up to be broken by the flow of change?"

Fifth Law of the Jungle

The Cage Door Is Open

We live in a cage. The cage is a perfect trap and yet its door is always open. We just don't realize it is open. We do our best to escape, but in trying to escape, we push the door further closed. The trap is perfect. If we would only stop pushing, if we would cease our attempts to escape, we would realize that the door was open all along.

We lead our lives in perpetual struggle, perpetual effort. But what are we struggling against other than the natural state of the world? All else has been created by man. If we stopped struggling, we would see the world for what it is and escape the trap, the trap we create for ourselves through our struggle. The door to the cage is always open.

the trap outside of us

We live in a box. Life for us is packaged in a box. We wake up in a boxy house or a boxy apartment and eat breakfast out of a box. We drive our boxy cars to our boxy offices and sit all day in front of our boxy monitors. We then drive our boxy vehicles or ride in our boxy train cars holding our boxy handheld devices, back to our boxy homes where we spend the rest of the day in front of boxy television sets. The box tells us who we are: It tell us what to think and believe. It tells us what we need and who we should fear and hate.

We are born free, but soon after we're taught to forget what we know and what we innately understand. We're taught that we belong in a box. We're ordained to the box of religion, a Christian box or a Muslim box or a Jewish box. And we are recruited to the box of a nation. We're taught that we're American or Indonesian or French or Chinese. We're taught that in some way we are different from each other and separate from the world. We're taught to take pride in insubstantial things, such as borders, ideals, and beliefs.

All creatures in nature live in accordance with the laws of the jungle. They are attuned to the world. They don't need invented methods to express what is within their spirits. They don't need invented boundaries to understand where they should live or invented necessities to know what they need to survive.

The **force of creation** has no name and no place. It is **within** us all; it is all.

The box we live in teaches us how to feel, it determines our self-worth, it teaches us the *man-made* laws. It cuts our wings so we remain restrained and conforming, still believing that we are living in a free world, as free as a bird—a bird with its wings severed.

In India, elephant trainers will tie a baby elephant to a tree for periods of time. The young elephant tries very hard to escape. He pulls and wriggles and jumps, yet the rope just tightens and the elephant remains shackled to the tree. Eventually, the elephant stops trying to escape and accepts his confinement. A couple of years pass and the elephant has become an adult, weighing several tons. The trainer continues to tie the elephant to the tree with the same rope he has always used. But the elephant believes that the rope is stronger than he is. Trapped by his conditioning, the elephant remains captive for life. To break free, all the elephant must do is eliminate the one limiting idea that he has been taught. The cage door is open.

Get out of the box, the cage. There is a vibrating universe out there where you truly belong.

You are a cosmic being. Claim your right to live in the real world, awe inspired.

The world is anything but a box. The world is round and has huge cavities filled with ocean waters, stretches of desert, belts of protruding mountains, and rivers that run through forests filled with creatures. It has poles and magnetic fields and atmosphere: it is a living thing.

We belong to the land. From it we came and to it we return.

The box is a cage we have built to protect us from the elements. We dwell in the illusory safety of the cage, afraid of the world we have alienated. We are trapped, like animals in a zoo. And we call this cage civilization—what an inappropriate term for it. People who live in the world live by the elements. They recognize the world for the living thing that it is. They do not resist the natural state of life. They have escaped the trap by accepting that it is a trap. They do not struggle against it.

the trap within us

The trap of the outer life is simply a reflection of the state of the inner life. If you are in the box on the outside, you are also in the box on the inside. Work with the traps within you and you will escape the traps outside of you.

We are so addicted to our ideals, beliefs, and concepts that we become trapped within them. All we have to do to escape is just let go.

the burmese monkey trap

In southern Myanmar some hill tribes still hunt monkeys for food. Monkeys are rather intelligent, and yet they are caught with a very simple trap. The hunters drill a hole in a coconut just large enough for a monkey to get a paw in. They fill the coconut with peanuts and tie it to a tree with wire. When a monkey smells the peanuts, he approaches the coconut. The monkey plays with the coconut, but the shape of the hole (a cone) makes it very difficult to get the peanuts out. So the eager monkey pushes its tiny paw in and manages to grab some of the peanuts. The monkey then tries to flee with his loot, but the coconut is tied to the tree. His paw filled with peanuts is too big to pull out of the coconut, and so he is trapped. In the morning, the hunter approaches. The monkey is terrified but cannot release itself from the trap. He cannot let go.

Inner life for most of us is life inside the conscious mind; there is no other life but that of the mind. We are trapped in our thoughts, our beliefs, our judgments, our ideas, ideals, and ideologies. Addicted to our concepts, abiding by the values instilled in us by "authorities," we refuse to give up what we have in our hands, yet we have nothing at all. We have a bunch of worthless peanuts, and we hold on to them as if they were the most precious stones. Let these peanuts drop and you will be released.

Poor creatures that we are, we have no moment of rest, no space for quiet, no emptiness. The mind is constantly busy, never at peace, never at rest, like an untuned radio. It has a life of its own, not abiding, not obeying. It seems that we are prisoners in our minds, for we live inside the box of the mind—limited, narrow, restraining. The jail of the conscious mind is perfection itself. The mind is the ultimate trap, a box filled with packaged beliefs and formulaic ideas. There is nothing new and fresh happening there, just more of the same, the grinding mundane existence deprived of the magic that we could experience.

Living in the tedious reality of our minds, many of us become so exhausted that we fall asleep. Asleep we live the rest of our lives. Sleep is such a temptation. It is easier to conform than to wake up, and the sleeping believe that they are wide awake.

But something is calling from deep within us, a remote voice still resonating from a distant world. We need perception; we need to wake up. Even asleep, we feel the pain of that exile—the pain of living not in accordance with our true nature, the pain of being isolated from our true selves, the pain of living in a false world. And we try everything we can to alleviate the pain, to find some solace for our longing souls. We try to escape our reality, but by pushing against it, we push the cage door closed. We seek an easy solution, a formulated one. We want to follow someone we believe has found an easy path to freedom. The desperation makes us gullible, and we buy the snake oil that promises hope.

To escape the trap, we have to work with what we have. We cannot buy someone else's solution, we must find our own way. No one can guide us.

Look inward, not outward. Expand your world by expanding yourself.

Go outside and sit and watch nature for a while. Sit under the night sky and realize for yourself that you are a cosmic being. It will make you feel different. Feel your way out of the box. Allow nature to undo you, let it heal you. Like a great therapist, nature will take care of you; you don't have to do anything at all—just let go, just be.

Abide by the laws of the jungle- the laws of nature—and things will be made easy. You are aligned innately to live in accordance with these laws. There is no effort involved, there's nothing to learn and nothing to achieve, nothing to do. Just be.

a key is clarity

What is your life? Do you lead a life of meaning or is life just happening to you? Are you reacting to circumstances or are you taking advantage of them? Are you sailing the seas of change, honing your navigation skills, and maintaining a course of integrity? Or are you as purposeful as a piece of rotten driftwood? Do you have clarity, tranquility, peace of mind? Without clarity, you are the driftwood.

Without clarity,
you lack purpose.
From clarity, one can
act with purpose.

We have been trained all our lives to react to circumstances, because people believe life happens to us, not for us. If life happens to you, you must react to it, constantly on the defensive. If life happens for you, you need only observe, contemplate, and align yourself with it. From observation and contemplation, understanding is born. From understanding comes clarity. From clarity grows right and purposeful action. We cannot be taught understanding. It is unique to each of us. But we can be taught observation and contemplation.

This process has a certain spiritual quality, for looking inside of oneself or contemplating the mundane is considered by man to be a spiritual activity. The word *spiritual* is too charged in many societies, and people find it difficult to explore any activity that is considered spiritual, particularly if it is not a part of an organized religion. This attitude is born from the false belief that there is a conflict between the spiritual and the mundane. Yet spirituality is nothing more than contemplation of the mundane. The *laws of the jungle* are spiritual as much as practical, for there is no separation between the practical and the spiritual. Life is sacred and spiritual, and the mundane is life.

Doubt what you were taught and observe for yourself, contemplating until understanding rises in you. This process is not owned by any religion. It is an innate ability that exists within each of us, and each individual has to walk the path alone. We are not puppets. We are not sheep led over the precipice by a blind shepherd. We are life itself.

another key is purpose

Life is teeming with meaning, yet we must determine the meaning for ourselves. We must find our own purpose through clarity. In the end, purpose is a choice. If you don't choose a purpose, a default purpose will be handed to you. This is the purpose of those who don't dare or don't know how to choose, who cannot find clarity. The default purpose is one of mediocrity, of living life within a man-made reality. It is the purpose of seeking only pleasure and avoiding all pain, playing it safe, living in a comfort zone. The source of this purpose is the conditioning we receive from the time we are born. Our civilized cultures cultivate this purpose.

But if we can achieve clarity, we can tune in to our true purpose. The most natural purpose, the purpose that exists within all of us, is to live life. It is the true purpose of all living things, and it is the most fulfilling purpose. On the most basic level, we must live life no matter what the circumstances.

To **live** life is to
meet each **circumstance**
with timely and **purposeful**
action. This is the
ultimate purpose.

Although we have been conditioned to abandon our true purpose, it still lies within us, waiting for a call to action. We have created a world separate from the natural world, a world full of illusions of safety and security, a world full of cages. Those illusions have dulled our senses, have made us believe that the true purpose is not enough, living life in its most natural form is not enough. We take life for granted.

Find your true and
natural purpose
and **align your
life** with it.
Your **struggle
will cease.**

accept the trap and escape

Stop trying to escape: it is futile. You will not achieve freedom through struggle, because struggle is part of the trap. When you try to break free you are only further trapped. The cage door is open but you are pushing it closed.

Certain things are achieved by effort and others are achieved by tuning in. If you try to escape the trap by means of effort, you will not have much rest in your life, and the box will consume you. If you tune in, if you accept, if you pursue clarity and purpose, escape is effortless.

Be discerning: there is a way out. You will have to find that way, your way, for yourself. No two walk the same way out, each one strides alone. Know that and you will never again be a follower, never be a slave to the box of civilization or the box of the mind. Though we cannot show each other the way, we can help each other along the path.

Accept that the **trap** is perfect and there is **nothing** you can do to escape it. Accept it and you will **relax**, you will **rest**.

Resting is a good beginning.

Don't push the door further closed. Freedom is achieved when you are free to be you.

Sixth Law of the Jungle

Evolution Is Created

The world is formed by a mysterious force that no one can describe. It transcends all dimensions and environments. Nothing can penetrate its realms. It is everywhere and in everything at all times. There is nothing but it.

The force of creation manifests itself through natural laws and systems, through evolution. There is no conflict between creationism and evolution.

Science and
spirituality are
part of the same
equation.

There is no need for this force to defy the natural laws that are emanating from it to begin with. The world exists, it functions, it evolves—that is miraculous.

The traditional conflict between creationism and Darwinism is a clear indication of the limitation of the isms. For millennia the religious and spiritual institutes held to the theory that the world was created exactly as it exists today by an entity they could identify and name. The intellectuals revolted against the man-made god and declared that there is no god, no creator, and that the laws of physics and mathematics can explain the creation of the world and the evolution of all species. These scientists became zealous and as narrow-minded as the clergy of the time.

Darwin was right, evolution is the ability of a species to constantly flow with change and adapt to circumstances. Those who adhere to the law of change survive. However, their adaptation and evolution is encoded in their design, which science alone cannot explain.

The sixth law of the jungle states that the world indeed is created by an omnipresent and omnipotent force beyond the ability of words to describe and explain. Yet this force manifests itself and its creation by systems and means that can be deciphered and measured.

creation guides evolution

I lived in the Amazon jungle for several years, working with different indigenous groups of people. Their intrinsic beauty and instinctive regard for nature persisted despite interference from the outside world. I stayed with them and learned by means of observation. Some of these natural laws I gathered from them, but I learned more from the Amazon itself.

The sixth law of the jungle presented itself to me clearly one day as I was strolling through the jungle with my very good friend and mentor Lazaro, the Takana shaman. He was sharing his knowledge with me about the flora and fauna. His sharp eyes never missed a detail, and he suddenly caught sight of a rare orchid in full bloom. We both stood in front of the flower in total reverence, for we could see the creator so clearly manifested in this flower.

The orchid looked like a wasp, down to the smallest possible detail. It had the shape of a wasp, the perfect dimensions of a wasp, the eyes of a wasp, the antennae of a wasp, and the fine wings of a wasp, crisscrossed with tiny mesh lines. It was a wasp. Except of course that it wasn't a wasp, it was an orchid. In this orchid I saw the face of the creator, and my eyes opened to see the miracles of the mundane.

You see, Darwin alone cannot explain that flower; his theory of adaptation to change, the survival of the fittest, can explain the mechanics of the flower but not the intelligence of it. The process of perfection through genetic manipulation, through trial and error, fails to recognize a truth that is so apparent. That process is guided by an underlying intelligence that guides all things and all beings.

The orchid has no mirror, no set of colored pencils. Nature produced that precise image of a wasp—its shape, color, and the fine details—from within. Here creation is apparent and one needs to be completely blind not to see that.

Life is a miracle.
  It is **naive**
      to confuse the
  explanation of life
  with the
creation of life.

the force of creation is evolution

The Amazon is home to some 50 percent of all living species, the true home for the majority of life on the planet. Living in the Amazon is a privilege. The competition for life in the jungle yields creativity and cooperation. The Amazon is a place of abundance, not scarce resources, and the competition is resolved by each species finding its unique niche, its relative advantage, and constantly improving it. How inspiring is that? And so each species finds its niche and these species naturally cooperate with each other to create an ecosystem, in which all are connected and interdependent. And through this cooperation, each species has room to evolve.

Evolution is the mechanics of creation, like physics and mathematics. It offers the means for us to explain the phenomena that manifest through change, but it cannot explain the source of life.

The world is created; the world is evolving.

Our existence is miraculous. The senses and the mind in our physical reality are what we have been given to understand and explain our existence. But we cannot rely on the senses and the mind. We cannot rely solely on science. Science is just scratching the surface of the mechanics of life. If we rely solely on it, we limit the scope of creation in our lives. Why try to limit a force so powerful, so beautiful?

If you want to realize the power of this force, observe nature. The mundane cannot hide it. It is within all things at all times. Let go of the concepts and ideals that have been given to you to explain your existence.

Observe life
not with your eyes and
not with your mind,
but with your
entire being.

Once you feel the creative power, you will understand. Let the force of creation guide you. Find your own relative advantage, your uniqueness, for it is not a weakness, it is your strength. Understand it, lean on it, and you will thrive.

Seventh Law of the Jungle

Life Is Perfectly Perfect

Creation is perfection. This perfection is all encompassing—it is everywhere and in everything. It is evident to the planet, to the seas and lakes, to the mountains and valleys, to the meadows and deserts, and to all living things.

Everything is at all times perfectly perfect.

Only one species is blind to the perfection. Only one species doesn't see the simple beauty of the laws of nature, but rather sees flaws and imperfections. Only one species is searching, confused and bewildered and not able to decipher the meaning of it all. And this species is vain, convinced that the world is the way they see and judge it to be. They fail to see that their world is the way they are, not the way it actually is.

We don't see the perfection of life because we view life with a limited perspective.

life is abundant

The truth is that there is enough of everything on this planet for everybody and on every level—an unlimited abundance of food, water, energy, space, peace, and good health. In this way, life is perfect. Nothing is lacking. Nothing except understanding and cooperation.

As human beings, we believe in scarcity, and in scarcity we live. We have been trained to believe that resources are limited. It is the concept of scarcity that has helped to create a culture based on competition instead of cooperation. Competition is one of the highest values in our society, and it is reflected in every aspect of our lives. We take pride in our competitiveness and yet competition yields aggression. Winning becomes all important, for that is the nature of competition. This leads to wars, atrocities, and pillaging. Greed has become our creed.

If we recognize that scarcity is just a misconceived perception, we open ourselves to cooperation. Through cooperation, we can make use of our relative advantages, the advantages we have gained through creation and evolution. Cooperation is the true nature of life on this planet, for we are all connected and interdependent.

The Amazon is the laboratory of life on earth. It is much more populous than our greatest city, yet no one goes hungry, no one needs social welfare to survive. Life is abundant and there is enough of everything for everyone. Some species are hunters and prey on others, yet there is no greed or malice. There is only natural balance.

In its perfection, life offers unlimited abundance.

If we accept that life is perfect and if we accept the abundance and stop competing for what we believe we need, we will accept our role in the greater ecosystem, the greater symphony.

But instead we convince ourselves that we need things that in reality are not necessary for happy and fulfilling lives. We believe these things are scarce. We believe we must compete for them. If we could only recognize that everything that life provides is everything that we need, we could cease our struggle. If we can trust that there is enough for everybody, we will achieve abundance-based cooperation, respectful management of the resources, a sense of harmony and balance that will prevail.

perfection is evident
through clarity

The truth of the perfection of life exists within us. We need only remember it. You are your own teacher, and all you need to learn is inside you. All you need is clarity and perspective to help you remember.

Clarity and perspective will come to you if you allow them to rise within you. Recall the importance of observation and contemplation. It is futile to will clarity and perspective into existence. They must come naturally from within you, and they will occur when you let go of the desire to control them.

Clarity must come first. If you are not clear, fear, confusion, and desperation will rule your life. You will cling to whatever materializes in your world and you will never recognize the perfection of life.

Accept that your
innate wisdom is
divine.

Don't let fear of the fog inside you drive you away. What you are searching for is behind the fog. Don't allow doubt and fear to nibble at your courage and trust.

Once you have regained clarity, you will be able to discover right perspective. Without right perspective, everything is personal, immediate, and inflamed. Without right perspective, it is the *I*, the *me*, and the *mine* that are controlling every aspect of your life. There is no room for the perfection that life has to offer.

Perspective is point of view, each individual's point of view. Remember that the world is not as it is, it is as you are. It is easy to see what you need to see and convince yourself that you have found right perspective. When you truly see the world as you are, you may be distraught at first, you may cry out and rage against it. But then you recognize it as a part of you, as you, and you will begin the journey to right perspective.

life is perfectly just

During one of my visits to Los Angeles, a car picked me up at the airport to drive me to my hotel. A newspaper awaited me on the backseat. Printed across the paper's front page was a shocking image: a Palestinian man carrying his dead eight-year-old son. The man's face expressed his immense grief. Looking at the image, I felt his suffering in my heart. I understood his was my suffering too.

Separation is illusion. One's suffering is the suffering of all, just as one's joy contributes to the joy of all. Injustice and atrocity are not isolated or regional. The whole is like the human body; if your hand is hurt, the rest of you is not indifferent to that local pain.

How can the world be perfectly perfect with all the suffering in the world, the wars, the atrocities, the hunger, and the injustices? Each injustice in the world is perfect because it awakens us more to the truth that the human experience, the global experience, is one. If we can understand and internalize this truth, it will lead us to harmony. It is perfect because it has to be perfect.

life is sacred
life is everything
everything is sacred

nature is always just

There is no injustice in nature; there are no victims and no atrocities; everything is perfectly perfect all the time. The storms are perfect and the droughts are perfect and the bush fires are perfect. The predators are perfect, and the prey is perfect, too.

As we know, everything constantly changes, and all things in their natural states agree with the flow of change. Nothing is permanent, all phenomena are in flux. In our living experience nothing is constant—emotions rise and pass away, feelings arise and cease, needs manifest and are met. Nothing whatsoever persists unless we resist.

Yet we believe our lives are full of injustice, because resisting is what we do best. We are never fulfilled and never at rest, always clinging, needing, aspiring, demanding, not accepting and not agreeable with change. What we want we never get, and if we get it, it is never enough, and when we get it, it is never in time. What we do not want comes to us all the time—it seems we are all victims by our own design. Any injustice that exists in our man-made world is man-made.

Yet all is perfectly perfect at all times. We have what we have. Tomorrow we may not have it any longer. We are who we are. Our uniqueness is our strength. The world is as we are. If we want the world to be different, as Gandhi said, we need to be that difference first.

We've forgotten how perfect we are, how perfect all human beings are. There is no need to save ourselves—we are perfect already. There is no need to save the world—the world is perfect as it is. The world cannot be anything but perfect; imperfection is impossible.

Like a black hole, so is the perfection of creation—nothing can escape it.

Eighth Law of the Jungle

The Time Is Now

There is no other time but now, the elusive present moment. The passage of time— the existence of the future and the past—is an illusion. The future is real only as you dream it in the present. The past is real only as you conjure it into the present.

Ask nature for the time. Ask a tree, ask a rock, ask a bird. You will see that they all have the same answer, that they are all synchronized to the universal clock, that they always have the exact and accurate time—the time, they will tell you, is NOW. A bird knows when and where to migrate. A fish knows when and where to spawn. The present is the most natural state for all living things because all other time exists in the mind only, it cannot be experienced.

If you want to live life,
live it now. Live it now
as if this moment
is all you have.
Live it now as if this
moment is eternal,
there is nothing but a
constantly unfolding now.

the future is an illusion

Tomorrow is only an assumption; it is a solid assumption, but it is still only an assumption. If the future is an illusion, falling in love with the future, becoming obsessed with the future, is insanity. If you rest all of your hopes and dreams on the future, seeking and searching for happiness, you deny the importance—the natural state—of the present. You deny yourself true joy. As the Buddha said, "We never know which comes first, death or tomorrow."

The **best** way to **prepare** for **tomorrow** is to **live today.**

Remove yourself from influences that threaten consequences or promise rewards for abiding by unnatural laws, for succumbing to fear. There is only one action, one experience, one moment that is valid—live life fully and fear-lessly *now*.

Be present and authentic.

For my thirtieth birthday, I went to the desert and chartered a Bedouin, Ali, to guide me through the wadis for ten days. We had many adventures and eventually became good friends. One day, after an intense sandstorm that was followed by very rare desert rains, Ali told me of a canyon deep in the wadi. "Maybe once in a decade, after heavy rains like these," he said, "the alcoves and nooks in the canyon fill with cool, fresh water you can drink and swim in." "We must go there," I told him, and we changed our route.

That night, we stopped in a small Bedouin encampment where Ali's cousin lived. He insisted we allow him to be our host. We prayed together, bowing and kissing the earth. Later we drank sweet tea and ate the steamed rice and fish we were served and talked about life in the world. We went to sleep filled with excitement, for in the morning, we would travel to the canyon.

In the morning, as we were preparing our camels, our host pulled Ali aside. They spoke for a few moments, and then Ali turned to me with a worried look in his eyes. He explained that his cousin had invited us to sit with him for the day and share his wild mutton from a recent hunt. In Ali's culture, to say no to hospitality and fresh meat were sacrilegious, an abuse of the ancient code. He simply could not refuse the offer. As my guide, he was very concerned about what my reaction would be, after all it was he that promised to take me to the magical canyon.

We stayed with his cousin all that day, seated around his simple hut over a tray of rice and mutton that had been cooked in the hot sand under a burning fire. The water in the nooks of the canyon remained as elusive as a dream. Ali taught me what every Bedouin innately knows, you live fully in the moment as it unfolds, nothing else is real.

The future lives only in the present, the past lives only in the present, there is nothing else. See this and see that the present always contains all possibilities, the present is eternal.

You cannot experience anything but the now. The future is alive and vibrant in the now.

life is in the present

The past is gone, for the experience of life is always now. What is past is not real anymore; it is only a story that you tell and the conclusions that you make. Both have very little to do with reality. Yet they are real because you carry them with you. They become a chain around your ankle. Cut the chains of the past—they are illusory.

Il fat mat, the Bedouins say. "The past is dead."

The future is in the making; each present moment contains all possibilities. Wake up and live among the living by experiencing the present and whatever it may bring. This is the natural way of experiencing life.

Don't wait.
Now is the time to be
courageous.

If you are fully engaged in what is, you are living. If you chase pleasant and happy experiences and have aversion to disturbance, you will never have a moment of rest, nor will you ever experience true joy. The art of living is not a quest for happiness, but rather a quest for happen-ness.

There is no use in fighting the present moment. Acceptance is a great virtue, for what is now cannot be changed. Don't blame others for what exists now; you are the co-creator of the present. Use this understanding as an empowering message to yourself. If you are responsible, you cannot be a victim. And if you are responsible, you can contribute to the now that will manifest in the future.

You can only create a future as a vision. Your purpose is to work toward the manifestation of your vision in the world, and you do it in the present. The secret of manifestation is not clinging desperately to the end result; it is casting a vision and letting it go. Asking for it and immediately giving thanks as if it was already given. Life is always present; past and future are realms of existence only in the now.

However, if you have no vision, if you've accepted a default vision thrust upon you by fear, you should examine your life and take responsibility for it. Remember, you are its co-creator.

Look at the present moment and accept it for what it is. If it feels harsh or difficult, just remember that just as you have helped create it you can help create a different next moment. With this outlook, the challenge will be intriguing, not overwhelming.

All faculties can experience the now except the mind. The body can feel things in the present, emotions can be experienced in the present, the spiritual elevation is the present. But the inclination of the mind is to think, to analyze the past and contemplate the future. That is the way we are designed. The mind needs to be engaged when thinking, when contemplation and analysis are needed. It is not the mind's function to constantly process worries and doubts. It is not the mind's purpose to chatter and flicker endlessly. You must teach yourself to cease the processing of your brain when it isn't necessary.

Simple actions, gradually, can bring you into the now. When you eat, eat. When you laugh, laugh. Be present and authentic about what you experience and you will get closer to the now. When in doubt, just ask yourself, "What is the time?" Don't look at a clock, find the answer within yourself or ask a tree or a passing bird for help, they will remind you.

"It's Now!"

Vesty Pakos, one of my best friends, gave me the best present a man could give. He initiated me in the now. He was a wild man, a well-known figure in the Andes and the Amazon, in cities and villages across Bolivia, where he lived. He was especially famous for his war cry, a full-lunged scream that he unleashed unexpectedly at any moment, at least twenty times a day. His cry was full of uninhibited exposure, for he would walk into any venue and put his hands to his mouth and shout his cry as loud as he could.

His war cry contained the essence of life, the essence of living in the present. It was a question and answer that explained it all.

Queste? Queste?

Vesty would only shout the question: Where is it? Where is it? But he was a famous man and his cry flew before him, never going unanswered: *Helaqui! Helaqui!* It is here! It is here! Someone would scream back.

The genius of this simple question is amazing. If
you listen carefully, you will hear another question and answer
curled like a hidden dimension inside the scream:

Where is it?

It is here!

When is it?

It is now!

It is all the same: the here, the now,
the present.

One night Vesty and I jumped out of a truck after a long journey from the Andes to the Amazon. It was after midnight and the small village we found ourselves in was sleeping. Vesty shook the dust from his clothes and raised his hands to the sides of his mouth. I cringed knowing what was coming. "Queste? Queste?" He screamed so loud the veins in his neck threatened to explode. But there was only the howl of a dog in response. We waited. Vesty raised his hands again and screamed so hard I thought I felt the ground tremble. "Where is it?" Then we heard a distant shout: "Helaqui! Helaqui!" And then another shout followed, and another one. It was magic. The whole village woke from its sleep. Men, women, and children came out of their huts with guitars and tambourines, with food and alcohol. We drank and ate and danced until sunrise. This is how Vesty Pakos lived his life, always there and then in the present.

Where is a better place than here, and when is a better time than now?

Scream your guts out if you need to, anything to wake yourself up. You are in a deep sleep, and you are only dreaming of the future and conjuring the past. Scream like Vesty until the world shakes.

Where is it?

It is here!

When?

Now!

Ninth Law of the Jungle

The Purpose of Life Is Death

L ife is a dangerous game. Simply and evidently, you die in the end. Trying to pretend life is safe—trying to play the game safely—is quite ridiculous.

If, on the other hand, you acknowledge death, you will play the game fully and completely, here in this moment. Life and death are like space and time—interrelated, interconnected, interdependent. To accept one is to accept the other. To deny one is to deny the other.

As space can only be experienced in time, life can only be experienced in death.

the continuum of life

There is no difference between life and death; they are not opposites, as we are taught to believe. They are both part of a single continuum, the continuum of life. Your current presence in this world, your personality, your ego, your history, your future—these are all just aspects of one episode on the continuum.

This life is not the **beginning** and death is not the **end**.

As human beings, our DNA contains the truth of the continuum. Yet the boundaries of our perception block our ability to understand it. When we are able to change our perception, we will see the truth.

This life that we perceive is only one dimension of the universe. It is foolish to believe it is the only dimension, that we are capable of understanding every possible dimension. It is equally foolish to believe we could comprehend all possible types of beings that could exist in this dimension and others. The shamans explore these mysteries to better understand this life. They pursue other dimensions, other beings. They pursue the spirit. Philosophers and scientists attempt similar pursuits, but they are reluctant to take the leaps of faith that are required to move beyond basic human perception.

While we are alive on these earthly plains, we hold to certain conceptions of the world based on our ability to perceive and explain. Each species perceives the world differently according to its faculties and senses. As humans, some of our faculties are very dull when compared to other species. However our mental faculty is superior to most other species. And so the human world is a world perceived by six senses: sight, touch, smell, taste, hearing, and mental perception. The mind is capable of creating its own concepts of the world—memories, visions, assumptions.

Yet even with this sixth sense- the mind—the capabilities of our senses are so limited. How can we perceive the truth of the world with such limitations? It is so easy to create an illusory world that seems real, so easy to deceive our senses. If our eyes cannot even perceive all the types of light that exist in our world, how can we trust our physical senses? If our mind creates false traps and misperceptions, how can we trust our mental faculties? We must move beyond these boundaries.

Our human faculties are dull and cumbersome when it comes to perceiving the subtle phenomena of life and death. Our senses are limited. We cannot see the real phenomena; we cannot penetrate the subtle realms by relying on our senses alone. Yet in our vanity we fail to accept that. We believe that what we cannot perceive does not exist, what we cannot perceive is an illusion. In fact the opposite is much closer to the truth.

What we perceive as real is the illusion; true reality waits beyond the reach of the six senses.

I lived and worked in the Amazon for years, and so when I decided to marry, I asked Doña Ema, the Pachamama priest of the Hymara, to conduct the ceremonies. And I asked Vesty Pakos, my best friend, to be my best man.

The wedding was celebrated in a remote location in the jungle, ten hours up river from the nearest jungle town. The following day, Vesty set out to return to the city. Another friend, Guillermo, asked if he could ride back with Vesty in his car. Vesty happily agreed. Before they left, Doña Ema grabbed Guillermo by the hand and whispered, "I saw his death hovering above him. You stay out of that car, stay in the town and get drunk." Guillermo dismissed the old witch and her nonsense.

They were still in the foothills of the Andes when Vesty cut a curve too fast and slid into the left lane to collide with a bulldozer. Guillermo was injured but survived the crash. Vesty died.

Doña Ema saw it all well before it happened, and she accepted—as did we all, eventually—that it was Vesty's time to go.

But Vesty did not go. For two weeks he visited daily with his friends and relatives. He let his presence be known in a variety of ways, but everybody agreed that it was him. The only person he did not visit was me. First I doubted the stories, and then I began to think that maybe Vesty was upset with me. It was my wedding that caused him to take the journey he didn't return from. I began to wish he would visit me. That very evening he came. Vesty came to take his last goodbye.

Many people think, There is nothing but what is familiar to me. When I die, this will be the end of it all, there is nothing beyond the reach of my knowledge. Yet there are billions of galaxies beyond the reach of our knowledge, and there may be hidden universes within each black hole. Why follow the example of an ostrich, pushing your head deep into a hole in the ground, oblivious to the world, stupefied and ignorant? The ostrich says, "It is so safe and cozy here." But life is death, safety is an illusion. Lift your head out of the hole, blow the dust of ignorance from your eyelids, and look at the emerging horizons.

Death is not the end, it is just a **beginning**. Our death is part of the design; immortality is beyond the **physical form**.

the gift of life

Ask yourself, "Who am I?" The true answer is the gift you have to offer in this life, and the gift this life has to offer to you. But who we are is far beyond what we are taught to hold on to.

Your actual life, as you live it now, is your gift to humanity and the evolution of the world.

The last shirt, it is said, has no pockets. And yet all your life you fill your pockets with fake treasures. They are not real, they will not last. That which is temporary, that which can change, is not real. Realize this truth and seek real treasures.

Who you are is a real treasure. You are not your name or titles or your image of yourself; you are not your profession or vocation; you are not your possessions. If you perceive all of these things as temporary, as disposable, you will be closer to the truth of who you are and what you have to offer this world.

It is all temporary—your youth, your health, your life itself. Why become attached to the things that are most perishable? If you are born, you will get old. Accept that and lose the vanity of youth. Its days are short as a season. If you are born, you will age and you will ail. Know that and lose the vanity of health. It will end. If you are born, you will age and you will ail and you will die. Accept that and lose the vanity of this life. It is but a passing episode.

Disassociate yourself from this story, this particular story that you are so involved with. When there is no story—no past, no future, no possessions—who are you then?

Disassociate yourself from what you think you are—the body, the feelings, the endless thoughts of the mind. Disassociate yourself from it completely and see a new path on the horizon, the path of the traveling soul. Be that soul, light and free, and your life will unfold along its true path. As you walk, it rises before you. Keep walking towards the light at all times, with grace and compassion, even through dark clouds. Undeterred, walk with faith and trust.

Disassociate yourself from the boundaries of traditions and education, your acquired nationality and taught religion. Disassociate yourself from current circumstances and particular stories and look for a truth that transcends time. Look for it in the ancient myths and in the source of all religions.

The truth of this life is compassion; be that compassion and you will be indestructible.

So who are we? We are traveling souls. Where are we? We are living this episode on the continuum of life. What is our purpose? We are drops within the great ocean. We are in this world, but not of it. We are traveling, passing through to evolve our spirits and those of others. Where did we come from, and where are we going? We come from the great ocean that is the whole of life, where there is no separation and all is one. We walk through this world with all of its illusions and temptations, struggling to make sense and find our true selves. Yet confusion reigns.

We exist like dust particles on the surface of the sphere that is Earth, and yet we are all connected to the source of life, where there is only one. Each of us is connected to that source now. We are enlightened, for there is nothing but that light. All we need is to awaken to that remembrance.

When we die, life does not end. Only our limited perception ends. When we die, we lose the drop consciousness and become one with the great ocean. Duality and separation is the nature of the illusion of this episode.

To overcome the illusion of separation, nurture compassion and act from that compassion.

the gift of death

The single most important moment of life is the moment of dying. And hence to die right is the greatest virtue. However, we never know when we will die. We must then live every day as if it was our last, and also without fear of death.

Buddha said, "We never know which comes first, death or tomorrow." That is how intimate a relationship we should have with death, as if it were only one night away. As if it were hanging around our shoulders.

It is.

Zorba was walking in the mountains when he encountered an old man planting a carob tree. "You foolish old man," intervened Zorba, "don't you know that it takes the carob seventy years to yield fruit?" "Oh, young man," replied the old man, "I live my life as if I'll never die." Awe inspired, Zorba was quiet for a moment. Then he said, "You foolish old man, I live every day as if it was my last."

In order to **die right**,
we have to live right.

In order to live **right**,
we have to **die right**.

It was my time to die, and I was solemn and nauseated and scared. I washed in the cold creek again and again, ready to be returned to the earth sacredly. I had chosen this death, yet my heart was beating hard and fast and my guts were quaking. Shaman Ignacio came to me, smiling and good-natured as always. He said it was a perfect day to die.

Ignacio was an old man. Yet he was truly alive, awakened, and enlightened, and this made him ageless. His grace was present in every stride he took, in every gesture he made. He carried a sense of sacredness about him, even as he dealt with the mundane. His sacred presence was balanced by a sense of lightness, of good humor and ease. His power radiated from his sinewy body, an unfathomable energy. He was lean and small, yet he could lift ten times the weight I could lift, he could walk for days and not tire, and he could maintain his energy on very little food. Even the natural elements seemed to flow off of him—the rain, the wind. He seemed to glide over the forest floor. At one with his surroundings, there was an unseen communication between his body and his environment.

"You are going to die now," he said.

"Hold to the courage and trust what is in your heart. Look fear in the eye, as awesome as it may be. Nothing can hurt you, you are indestructible."

We sat by an old buttress tree, the smell of fresh rot steaming off the jungle floor nauseated me and I had to focus on my breath to regain my composure. Ignacio was as remote as a stranger. Doubt rushed into my mind, for doubt is always ready to bite, injecting its poisonous venom. I avoided the bite. I relied on my breath and a vision of light.

Ignacio made the necessary preparations. He spread a roughly woven mantle on the earth and placed a short machete and a hollowed cane on it. He then lifted the machete in his hand. "What a blessed day. It is your time to be sacrificed; your life will end now. I will slay you here under this old tree today, just as your forefather Abraham slaughtered his children, Ishmael and Isaac. Only in your death will ignorance cease."

He looked at me and his eyes were soft and remote. I knew I would trust my life to him, let him slay me. The ignorant are the walking dead, so what did I have to lose? Nothing. I rested my head on the forest floor. Ignacio lifted the machete above my head and chanted in the old language of the Uchupiamona, a tribe, now extinct, that once lived by the Tuichi River. "This knife will cut any thread of life that holds you to this plane." He laid the knife by my head and picked up the hollow cane. "This cane will connect you to the heavens above. May you travel to the light and may you be resurrected here with me again."

He poured a small amount of yellow powder into the cane, brought it to my nose, lifted my chin, pressed the end of the cane tight against my nostrils, and blew the powder into me. I was sent on a journey like an atomic explosion.

First came blazing pain and a sharp odor that burned my sinuses. Then I began to lose control, overwhelmed by nausea, fear, panic. Addicted to the familiar, all I wanted was to hold on to it. Where was Ignacio now? Suddenly I saw him approach with the machete raised in his hand, chanting. In his eyes I saw the kill. He struck me down with all his might. I felt my head fall off and roll down the roots of the tree. I was gone now, dead, my body left behind like baggage, a package of flesh, a carcass.

I was swept inside a tumbling whirlwind, moving fast towards the eye of the storm. It was sucking me in. The fear was still present. Then I saw Ignacio again, he was still, like a statue, leaning on his cane with a serene smile on his face. "Let go," he told me without opening his mouth or uttering any sound at all. "Let go, don't hold on to anything." And he disappeared. His words echoed like thunder in a canyon. There was an explosion of light, and everything became completely still in sacred silence. A new realm opened to me and I embarked.

Like stepping off the gangway of a ship after a long journey at sea, my steps were careful and measured. I was the eternal traveler, and this was my home. Everything was new, yet familiar. It all made perfect sense, no explanations were needed. I was imbued with a strong sense of belonging and understanding. The stillness was soothing. It was light, and in that light I was enlightened. No separation, no delusions, no sorrow, no stories, only pure sacred life. I was home again, where I came from and where I would return. Everything had happened already and was happening now and forever. There was no fear, no desperation, no hope, no doubt—just trust and gratitude and the light of endless love and compassion. There was no need to search; nothing had been lost. Everything was perfectly perfect.

On that forest floor I died and was born again. The light was soft, the air was warm, and the stillness transcended to this life. Every leaf was illuminated and sacred. I was back in that useless parcel, in my body, like Lazarus arisen from death. The top of my head pulsated and knowledge permeated my mind. I knew it all; I knew everything there is to know, and the light of wisdom shone through me.

Ignacio was there with a bowl of water in his hands to baptize me and to quench my thirst. His face was beaming with light and laughter and the joy of endless compassion. He brought the water to my mouth with his hands and touched my lips.

"My lips will praise and utter prayer," is the first thing I said to him.

"There is no paradise there; for paradise is here now. And there is no hell there, for Satan walks among us. Wake up from your long hibernation, blow the dust off your eyelids, and dare to lift the veil of ignorance."

the gift of karma

Imagine that when this episode ends, when you die, you can see your life, play it forward and backward like a movie. You see yourself try to hide who you really are, try to hide what you are truly doing, what's truly in your heart, you try to hide from others and from yourself. You hide without realizing there is nowhere to hide. All of your actions, all of your intentions, are awash in a bright light, revealed and recorded in the continuum forever. Be the protagonist and the observer at the same time.

Some call it karma, others call it heaven and hell. Yet most people understand that this life is not the end, that death is not the end, and how we behave in this life has an effect on how we will go on, an effect on the next episode on the continuum.

Life is not perishable; it is sacred and eternal.

Death is the disposal of the form, the body. Possessions, religion, and nationality are left like a pile behind. Associate yourself with truth of life, with the continuum, and live forever. And knowing that you will live forever, be discerning. What can you take with you? Which of your faculties can be honed and transferred? How do you strive for your full potential, for the full scope of your destiny in this and every moment of life?

The last shirt has no pockets, so why invest in the perishable when you can invest in the indestructible. Walk the path, the winding path of eternal life, with elegance and humility, with courage and purpose. Abide to compassion and kindness and harmonious ways in your thoughts, speech, actions, and intentions. Avoid aversion and attachment to the illusions of this life and be born to immortality.

In death, life does not end. Life is energy, and energy is converted. In death, the energy of life is transformed. In the act of dying you give the gift of consciousness to the next episode, to the next life. You are responsible for the evolution of your spirit. If your consciousness at the moment of death is one of fear, confusion, bitterness, and disenchantment, that will be your gift to the next life. If you are serene, centered, maintaining right perspective, and filled with sacred awe, that will be your contribution to the evolution of your spirit.

What you are in death is your gift to the evolution of the world and to the next episode on the continuum of life.